SCORE!

Mountain Challenge

MATH WORKBOOK

KAPLAN

PUBLISHING

New York

This publication is designed to provide accurate and authoritative information in regard to the subject matter covered. It is sold with the understanding that the publisher is not engaged in rendering legal, accounting, or other professional service. If legal advice or other expert assistance is required, the services of a competent professional should be sought.

Contributing Editor: Justin Serrano
Editorial Director: Jennifer Farthing
Editorial Development Manager: Tonya Lobato
Assistant Editor: Eric Titner
Production Editor: Dominique Polfliet
Production Artist: Creative Pages, Inc.
Cover Designer: Carly Schnur

Published by Kaplan Publishing, a division of Kaplan, Inc.
888 Seventh Ave.
New York, NY 10106

Printed in the United States of America

May 2007
10 9 8 7 6 5 4 3 2 1

ISBN-13: 978-1-4195-9466-3
ISBN-10: 1-4195-9466-4

Kaplan Publishing books are available at special quantity discounts to use for sales promotions, employee premiums, or educational purposes. Please email our Special Sales Department to order or for more information at *kaplanpublishing@kaplan.com*, or write to Kaplan Publishing, 888 Seventh Avenue, 22nd Floor, New York, NY 10106.

Table of Contents

How to Use Your *SCORE! Mountain*
Challenge Workbook . . . . **iv**

Time to Get Organized and
Learn to Use Your Time Wisely! . . . . **vii**

SCORE! Mountain Challenge
Online Instructions . . . . **xii**

Base Camp 1: Shapes and Measurement **1**

Base Camp 2: Number Sense **25**

Base Camp 3: Probability and
Data Interpretation **49**

Base Camp 4: Fractions. **75**

Base Camp 5: Algebra and Number Patterns **99**

Base Camp 6: Everyday Math **123**

Tools **147**

Are you ready for a fun and challenging trip up *SCORE!* Mountain?

Getting Started

This exciting workbook will guide you through 6 different base camps as you make your way up *SCORE!* Mountain. Along the way to the top you will get to challenge yourself with over 120 math activities and brain teasers.

To help you figure out the answer to each question, use the blank space on the page or the extra pages at the back of your workbook. If you need extra space, use a piece of scrap paper.

Base Camp

SCORE! Mountain is divided into 6 base camps—each covering an important mathematics topic—and meets the educational standards set forth by the National Council of Teachers of Mathematics (NCTM). The final base camp in this workbook, Everyday Math, has a special focus on the many ways we might use mathematics each day.

Your trip through each base camp will take you through 15 questions related to the base camp topic, a Challenge Activity designed to give your brain extra practice, and a 5-question test to see how much you've learned during your climb.

Each question comes with helpful hints to guide you to the right answer. Use these hints to make your climb up *SCORE!* Mountain a great learning experience.

The Answer Hider

Try your best to answer each question before looking at the answer. Included in the back of this workbook is a *SCORE!* answer hider that you can tear out. Use the answer hider to cover up the answers as you work on each question. Then, uncover the answer and see how well you did!

Celebrate!

At the end of each base camp there's a fun celebration as a reward for making it through. It's your time to take a break before going to the next base camp.

SCORE! Mountain Challenge Online Companion

Don't forget—more fun waits for you online! Each base camp comes with a set of 10 online questions and activities, plus a mountain-climbing study partner who will encourage you and help you track your progress as you get closer to the top of *SCORE!* Mountain.

The *SCORE!* online base camps are designed to match the base camps from the workbook. As you reach the end of each base camp in the workbook, we encourage you to go to your computer to round out your *SCORE!* Mountain Challenge experience. Plus, after you successfully complete the last online base camp, you are awarded a Certificate of Achievement.

Certificate of Achievement

When you complete the entire workbook and online program you will receive your very own Certificate of Achievement that can be shared with family and friends!

Time Management

In addition to all of the great mathematics practice that your *SCORE! Mountain Challenge Workbook* has to offer, you'll find lots of helpful tips at the front of the workbook on how you can best organize your time so that you can do well at school, get all of your homework and chores done, and still have time for fun, family, and friends. It's a great way to help you perform at your best every day!

Tools

Every mountain climber needs a set of tools to help him or her reach the mountaintop. Your *SCORE! Mountain Challenge Workbook* has a special set of tools for you. In the back of your workbook you'll find a handy guide to help you get through each base camp. You can use these tools whenever you need a helping hand during your climb up *SCORE!* Mountain.

Enjoy your trip up *SCORE!* Mountain. We hope that it's a fun learning experience!

GOOD LUCK!

Learning can be hard work!

Here are some helpful tips.

Keep track of time!

What are you doing today?

Circle the pictures!

Monday	Tuesday	Wednesday	Thursday	Friday
School	School	School	School	School
Sports	Sports	Sports	Sports	Sports
Music	Music	Music	Music	Music
Dance	Dance	Dance	Dance	Dance
Play	Play	Play	Play	Play
Home	Home	Home	Home	Home

How do you start your day?

Circle the pictures!

TODAY	
Wake up!	
Get clean	
Get dressed	
Eat breakfast	
Off to school!	

SCORE! *Mountain Challenge*

What do you do after school?

Circle the pictures!

Monday	Tuesday	Wednesday	Thursday	Friday
Snack	Snack	Snack	Snack	Snack
Homework	Homework	Homework	Homework	Homework
Fun and play!	Fun and play!	Fun and play!	Fun and play!	Fun and play!

How do you help at home?

Chores are important!

What chores do you do at home to help?

Color the pictures!

Remember to make time for fun!

Make time for your friends and family.

Color the pictures!

Your *SCORE! Mountain Challenge Workbook* comes with a fun, interactive online companion. Parents, go online to register your child at **kaptest.com/scorebooksonline**. Here your child can access 60 exciting math activities and a cool mountain-climbing study partner.

Children, when you log on, you'll be brought to a page where you will find your *SCORE! Mountain Challenge Workbook* cover. You'll also be asked for a **password**, which you will get from a passage in this workbook. So have your workbook handy when you're ready to continue your *SCORE!* Mountain Challenge online, and follow the directions.

Good luck and have fun climbing!

Base Camp

1

Shapes and Measurement

Are you ready to begin climbing *SCORE!* Mountain? Let's get started. **Good luck!**

SCORE! MOUNTAIN TOP

BASE CAMP 5

BASE CAMP 4

BASE CAMP 3

BASE CAMP 2

BASE CAMP 1

1. How many circles? **Circle** the number.
Color them!

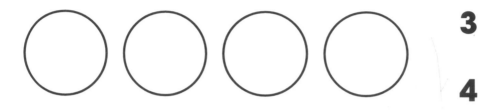

3

4

Hint #1:	3 cats

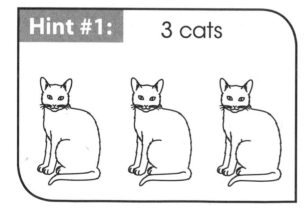

Hint #2:	4 shoes

Answer:

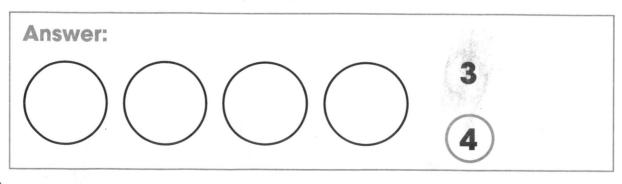

3

(4)

2. How many squares? **Circle** the number. **Color** them!

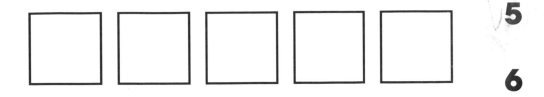

5

6

Hint #1:   5 boats

Hint #2:   6 hands

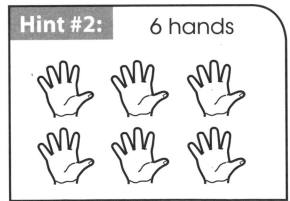

Answer:

⑤

6

3. How many rectangles? **Circle** the number. **Color** them!

7

8

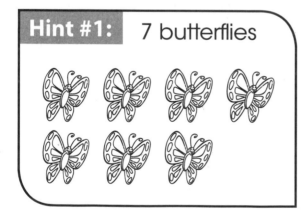

Hint #1: 7 butterflies

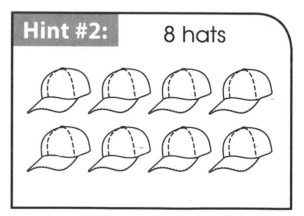

Hint #2: 8 hats

Answer:

7

⑧

4. How many triangles? **Circle** the number. **Color** them!

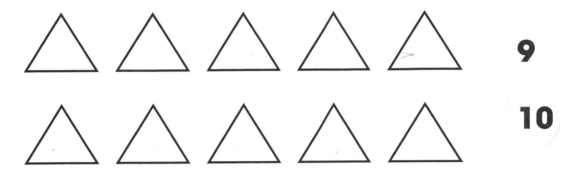

9

10

Hint #1: 9 books

Hint #2: 10 cakes

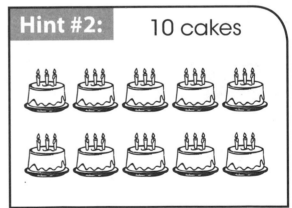

Answer:

9

(10)

5. How many **sides**?

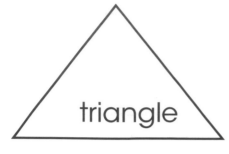

triangle _____ _ _ _ _ _____

rectangle _____ _ _ _ _ _____

square _____ _ _ _ _ _____

Hint #1:

Hint #2:

Count one side at a time!

Answer:

A triangle has **3** sides.

A rectangle has **4** sides.

A square has **4** sides.

© Kaplan Publishing, Inc.

6. Let's **color** and **count**!

Make **triangles** <u>**blue**</u>.

Make **squares** <u>**yellow**</u>.

Make **rectangles** <u>**green**</u>.

Make **circles** <u>**red**</u>.

How many **circles**? _____

How many **squares**? _____

How many **rectangles**? _____

How many **triangles**? _____

Hint #1:	Hint #2:
Do you see the triangles in the sun?	Use the right colors!

Answer: How many **circles**? **1**

How many **squares**? **2**

How many **rectangles**? **2**

How many **triangles**? **9**

7. **Same** shape or **different** shapes? **Put** an **X** next to the word that you think is true.

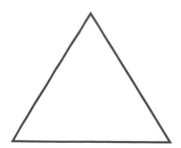 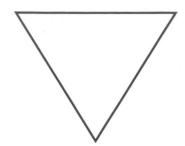

Same ____

Different ____

Hint #1:

Count the sides. Do they have the same number of sides?

Hint #2:

Turn the book **upside down**! Do they still look the same?

Answer:

Same __X__

Different _____

They are the **same shape**! The triangle on the **right** is just upside down.

© Kaplan Publishing, Inc.

8. Let's try again! Same shape or **different** shapes? **Put** an **X** next to the word that you think is true.

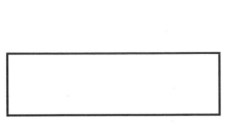

Same _____

Different _____

Hint #1:
Count the sides. Do they have the **same** number of sides?

Hint #2:
Do they look the **same** to you?

Answer:

Same ___X___

Different _____

They are the **same shape**!
They are both **rectangles**.
They are both the **same size**.
One is **turned**.

© Kaplan Publishing, Inc.

9. One more time! **Same** shape or **different** shapes?
Put an **X** next to the word that you think is true.

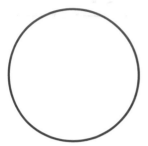 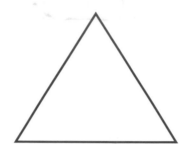

Same ____

Different ____

Hint #1:

Count the sides. Do they have the **same** number of sides?

Hint #2:

Do they look the **same** to you?

Answer:

Same _____

Different __X__

They are **different shapes**!
The one on the left is a **circle**.
The one on the right is a **triangle**. They are **different**!

10. Look at the **train**.

How many **rectangles**? _ _ _ _ _

How many **squares**? _ _ _ _ _

How many **circles**? _ _ _ _ _

Hint #1:

□ □ □ □
1 2 3 4

= **4 squares**

Hint #2:

○ ○ ○ ○ ○ ○ ○ ○
1 2 3 4 5 6 7 8

= **8 circles**

Answer:

□ □ □ □ = **4 squares**

= **4 rectangles**

○ ○ ○ ○
○ ○ ○ ○ = **8 circles**

11. **Trace** the solid shapes.

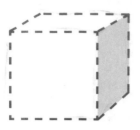 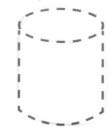 

Cube   **Cylinder**   **Cone**

Can you find some things that have these shapes?
Write your answers.

_____

Cube _____
_____

Cone _____
_____

Cylinder _____

Hint #1:   cone

Hint #2: Keep looking!   cube

Answer: Here are some items you might have found:

 Cube   **Cone**   **Cylinder**

dice   ice cream cone   can

12. Let's **compare**! **Circle** the **biggest** square.

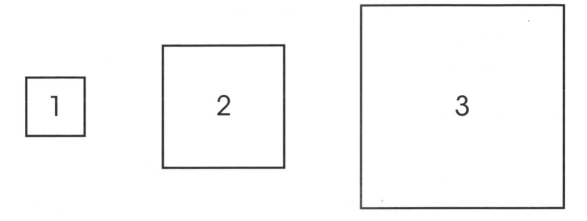

Hint #1:

biggest

Hint #2:

biggest

Answer:

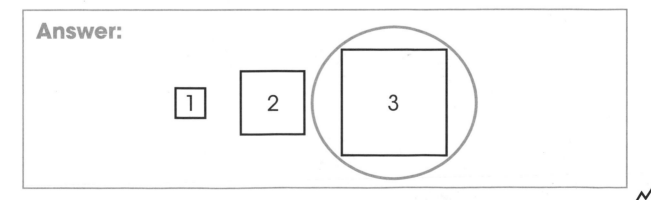

13. Who is the **tallest**?
Circle the **tallest** child.

Hint:

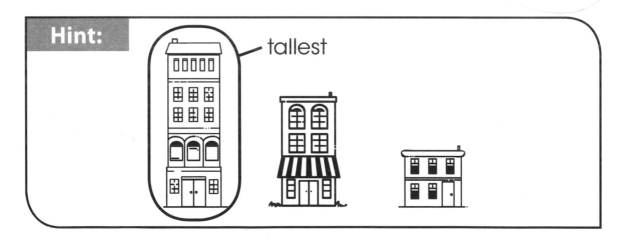

tallest

Answer:

14. Which is the **shortest**?
Circle the **shortest** dog.

Hint:

shortest

Answer:

15. Circle the right answer.

Which is **longer**, your **arm** or your **leg**?

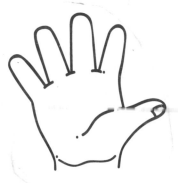 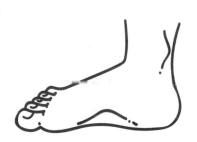

Which is **smaller**, your **hand** or your **foot**?

Hint #1:

Put your **arm** next to your **leg**. Which is **longer**?

Hint #2:

Put your **hand** next to your **foot**. Which is smaller?

Answer:

Your (leg) is **longer** than your arm.

Your (hand) is **smaller** than your foot.

You're doing a great job so far!
Are you ready for a Challenge Activity?
Good luck!

Here are some **solid shapes**.

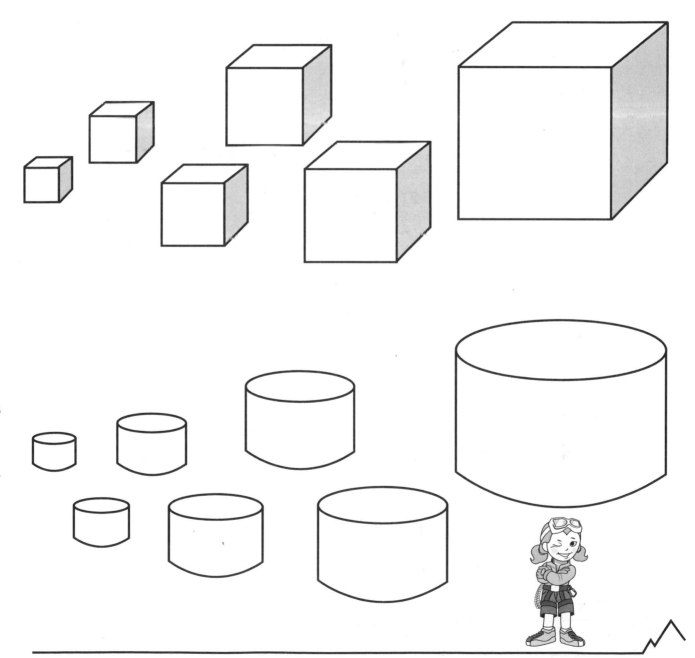

a) Circle the **biggest cube**.

b) Put an **X** through the **smallest cylinder**.

c) Are there **more** or **less** cylinders than cubes?
Circle your answer.

Hint #1:

First **count** the **cubes**.
Then **count** the
cylinders.

Hint #2:

Are there **more cubes**
or **more cylinders**?

Answer:

a) Here's the **biggest cube**:

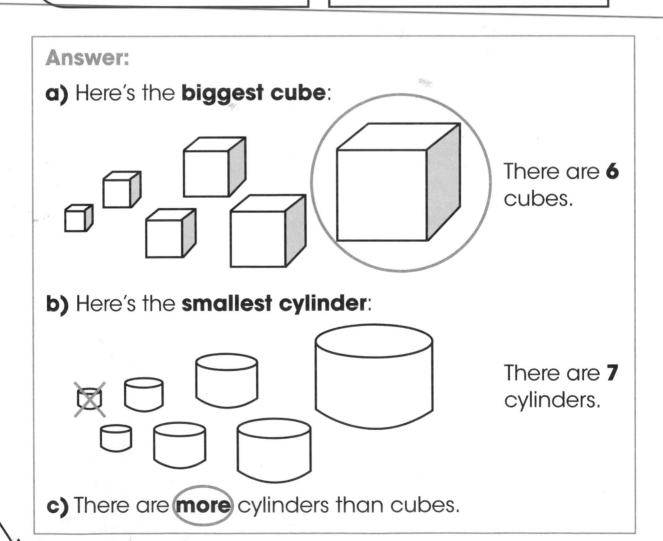

There are **6** cubes.

b) Here's the **smallest cylinder**:

There are **7** cylinders.

c) There are (**more**) cylinders than cubes.

Let's take a quick test and see how much you've learned during this climb up *SCORE!* Mountain. Good luck!

1. Draw a shape with **4 sides**.

4 sides _____

2. Draw a shape with **3 sides**.

3 sides _____

3. Circle the **rectangles**.

4. Louisa lost **4** teeth.
DeShawn lost **6** teeth.
Who lost **more** teeth?
Circle your answer.

Louisa

DeShawn

5. **Circle** the **tallest** building. Put an **X** through the **shortest** building.

Building A

Building B

Building C

Answers to test questions:

1. A **rectangle** and a **square** both have **4 sides**.

2. A **triangle** has **3 sides**.

3. Did you find all the rectangles?

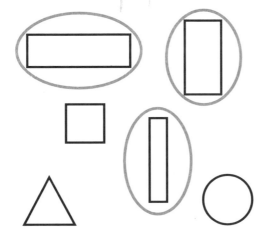

4. **Deshawn** lost more teeth than Louisa.

5. **Building C** is the **tallest**.
Building A is the **shortest**.

Celebrate!

Let's take a fun break before we climb up to the next base camp. You've earned it!

Let's play **shape search!**

Play with a friend or family member and see who can find the most things that are shaped like **squares, circles, rectangles,** and **triangles**!

Congratulations! You're on your way up *SCORE!* Mountain.

BASE CAMP **1**

Here are the shapes to look for:

square

circle

triangle

rectangle

These shapes can be found all over. A book can be a **rectangle**, a slice of pizza can be a **triangle**, and even your television is a **shape**!

See who can find the **most** things that are each shape. The person who finds the most shapes is the **shape search winner**!

Good luck and have fun! You deserve it for working so hard!

1. Trace the numbers 1-10.

Hint #1:

Be careful! **Stay** on the **dotted lines**.

Hint #2:

Say each number as you trace!

Answer:

1 2 3 4 5
6 7 8 9 10

2. Now, **write** the numbers **backward** from **10–1**.

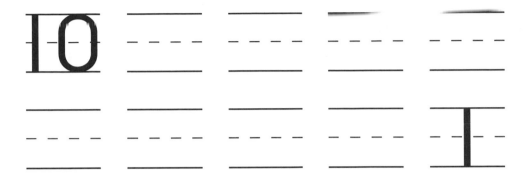

Hint #1:

What comes **before** 10? Keep going backward!

Hint #2:

Try **counting** backward from **10–1** out loud. Does that help?

Answer:

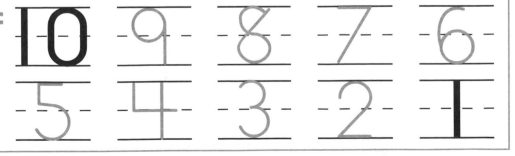

10 9 8 7 6
5 4 3 2 1

3. Circle the racecar that is <u>first</u>.

Put an **X** on the racecar that is <u>second</u>.

Put a **line** through the racecar that is <u>third</u>.

Hint:

First = **1st**
Second = **2nd**
Third = **3rd**

Answer:

4. Count the elephants!

_____
- - - - - - - -
_____ elephants

Now, **count** the giraffes!

_____
- - - - - - - -
_____ giraffes

Are there **more** elephants or giraffes?

_____
- -
_____

Hint:

Which number is bigger?

Answer:

There are **6** elephants.

There are **7** giraffes.

There are **more giraffes** than elephants.

5. All about you!

How many **eyes** do you have? _____

How many **ears** do you have? _____

How many **fingers** do you have? _____

Hint #1:

Look at yourself
in the mirror.

Hint #2:

How many **eyes** do you have?
How many **ears** do you have?
How many **fingers** do you have?

Answer: Everyone is different!

Most people have **2 eyes**.

Most people have **2 ears**.

Most people have **10 fingers**.

6. **Circle** the basket with **8** loaves of bread.

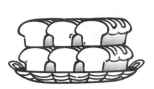  

Hint #1:

Count the loaves in each basket!

Hint #2:

Here are **8** coins. Which basket has the **same** amount of loaves of bread?

Answer:

7. Circle 7 of the children.

Hint #1:

There are **10** children pictured. **10** is **more** than **7**.

Hint #2:

If you want to circle **7** of the **10** children, how many children will **not** be circled?

Answer:

Here is one possible answer.

8. Let's **add**!

Draw 3 balloons.

Draw 1 more balloon.

How many **total** balloons did you

draw? _____

Hint #1:
Count **3** balloons plus **1** more balloon, and you will have your answer!

Hint #2:
3 + 1 = ?

Answer: Draw 3 balloons.

Draw 1 more balloon.

How many **total** balloons did you draw?

3 balloons + 1 balloon = 4 balloons

9. How many lollipops are left?

$$4 \quad - \quad 3 \quad = \underline{\hspace{6cm}}$$

Hint #1:

Use your **pencil** and draw **4** lollipops. Then erase **3** lollipops. How many are left?

Hint #2:

4 − 3 = ?

Answer: You would have just **1** lollipop left!

4 − 3 = 1

10. How many dogs are here?

2 + 1 = ‑ ‑ ‑ ‑ ‑ ‑ ‑ ‑

Hint:

What do you get when you add **2** and **1**?

Answer:

2   +   1   =   3 dogs

11. How many kids are here?

$$4 \quad + \quad 5 \quad = \quad \text{_____}$$

Hint:

What do you get when you add **4** and **5**?

Answer:

$$4 \quad + \quad 5 \quad = \quad 9 \text{ kids}$$

12. How many cars are left?

$$6 - 3 = \text{_____}$$

Hint #1:

What do you get when you **take away** **3** from **6**?

Hint #2:

Draw **6** cars in pencil. Then erase **3** of them. How many cars are left?

Answer:

$$6 - 3 = \text{3 cars}$$

13. How many boats are left?

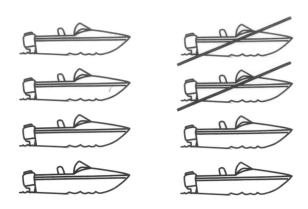

8   −   2   =   _____

Hint #1:

Draw **8** boats **in pencil**. Then erase **2** of them. How many boats are left?

Hint #2:

What do you get if you have **8** and you *take away* **2**?

Answer:

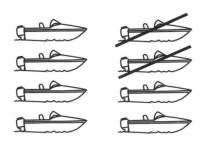

8   −   2   =   6 boats

14. Time to **add**!

$$2 + 4 = \underline{}$$

$$3 + 1 = \underline{}$$

$$3 + 3 = \underline{}$$

$$1 + 7 = \underline{}$$

$$6 + 3 = \underline{}$$

Hint #1:
Use your fingers to help you count!

Hint #2:
Count out loud if it helps!

Answer: $2 + 4 = 6$
$3 + 1 = 4$
$3 + 3 = 6$
$1 + 7 = 8$
$6 + 3 = 9$

15. Time to **subtract**!

$$5 - 2 = \underline{\hspace{3em}}$$

$$3 - 1 = \underline{\hspace{3em}}$$

$$8 - 4 = \underline{\hspace{3em}}$$

$$6 - 5 = \underline{\hspace{3em}}$$

$$7 - 2 = \underline{\hspace{3em}}$$

Hint #1:

Remember, you can use your fingers to help you count!

Hint #2:

Remember, sometimes it helps to say the problems out loud.

Answer: 5 – 2 = **3**
3 – 1 = **2**
8 – 4 = **4**
6 – 5 = **1**
7 – 2 = **5**

Challenge Activity

You're doing a great job so far!
Are you ready for a Challenge Activity?
Good luck!

Li's flowers:

Dan's flowers:

Kelly's flowers:

a) Who has the **most** flowers?
Circle the answer.

Li   Dan   Kelly

b) Who has the **least** flowers?
Circle the answer.

Li   Dan   Kelly

c)

Hint #1:

5 + 5 = ?

Hint #2:

4 + 2 = ?

Answers to Challenge Activity:

a) Li has the **most**. She has **10 flowers**!

b) Kelly has the **least**. She has **6 flowers**!

c) 🌼 🌼 + 🌼 🌼 + 🌼 🌼 = **6 flowers**

Let's take a quick test and see how much you've learned during this climb up *SCORE!* Mountain. Good luck!

1. Write the numbers **1–10**.

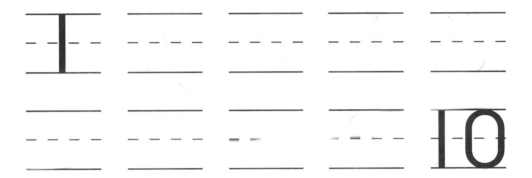

2. **Circle** the cake with **6** candles.

3. Maggie had **3** stickers. She gave **1** to Tyrone. How many are left?
Circle your answer.

4 stickers

3 stickers

2 stickers

1 sticker

4. 4 + 5 = ____

5. 8 − 3 = ____

Answers to test questions:

1.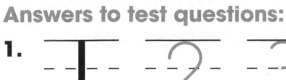

2.

3. 4 stickers

3 stickers

2 stickers

1 sticker

3 − 1 = 2

4. 4 + 5 = **9**

5. 8 − 3 = **5**

Celebrate!

Let's take a fun break before we go to the next base camp. You've earned it!

Connect the dots!

What is the secret picture?

Congratulations! You're getting closer to the top of *SCORE!* Mountain.

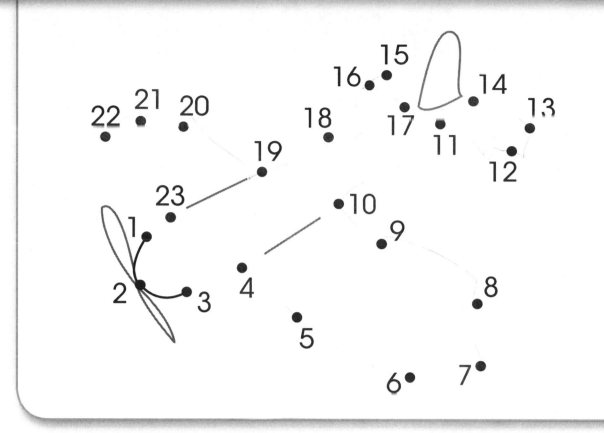

Good luck and have **fun**! You deserve it for working so hard!

Base Camp 3

Probability and Data Interpretation

Are you ready for another fun climb up *SCORE!* Mountain? Let's get started! Good luck!

SCORE! MOUNTAIN TOP

BASE CAMP 5

BASE CAMP 4

BASE CAMP 3

BASE CAMP 2

BASE CAMP 1

1. Jen has a favorite **toy car**. Guess which one it is! Follow the clues!

Clue #1: No writing
Clue #2: Two doors
Clue #3: Square windows

Circle Jen's favorite toy car.

Hint #1: Look for clues!

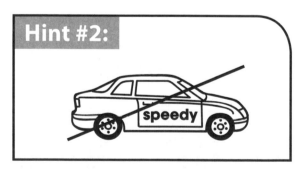

Hint #2:

Answer:

2.

How are the dogs grouped?
Circle your answer.

color   **size**

Hint #1:

Some are **big**:

Hint #2:

Some are **small**:

Answer: The dogs are grouped by (size).

small   **big**

3. You have **1 penny** and **1 quarter**.

You **drop** them. What is **not** possible?
Circle your answer.

A.

C.

B.

D.

Hint #1:

You have **1 penny**.

Hint #2:

You have **1 quarter**.

Answer: B is right!

4. Here are **6 lions** and **3 bears**.

Are there **more lions** or **more bears**?
Circle your answer.

Hint #1:

Which is **bigger**:
6 or **3**?

Hint #2:

The **bigger** number
means that there are
more of them.

Answer: There are **more lions** than bears.

5. Which are you **most likely** to pick?

Circle your answer!

Hint #1:

Which is **more**: **5 bananas** or **1 apple**?

Hint #2:

Which number is **bigger**: **5** or **1**?

Answer: You are **most likely** to pick a **banana**.

But you could still pick an **apple**!

6. Which are you **most likely** to pick first?

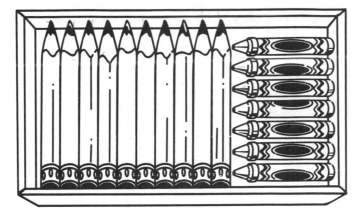

Circle your answer!

© Kaplan Publishing, Inc.

Hint #1:

Which is **more**:
10 pencils or
7 crayons?

Hint #2:

Which number is
bigger: **10** or **7**?

Answer: You are **most likely**
to pick a **pencil**.

But you can still pick a **crayon**!

7. Look at this spinner. Which color are you **least likely** to land on?

_____

- -

_____

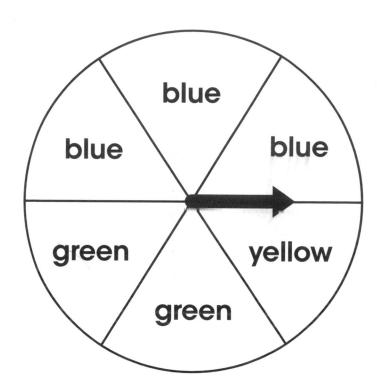

Hint #1:
Count each color.

3

2

1

Hint #2:
Which is the **smallest**: **3**, **2**, or **1**?

Answer: The spinner would have the **least** chance of landing on **yellow**.

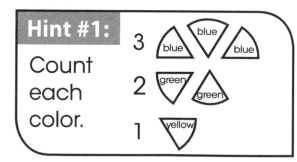

8. Alex spun the spinner **10 times**. Here are his results:

yellow: **2** times
blue: **5** times
green: **3** times

Here is a **graph**:

Which **color** did he spin the **most**?

_____

_ _ _ _ _ _ _ _ _ _

_____

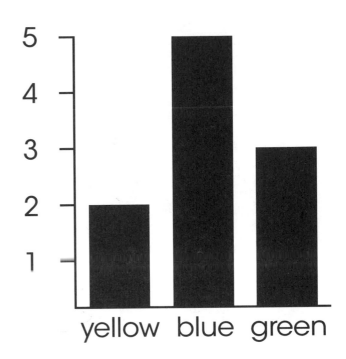

yellow blue green

Hint #1:

Which is **tallest**?

Hint #2:

Which number is the biggest: **2**, **5**, or **3**?

Answer: **Blue** was spun the **most**. He spun blue **5 times**.

9. 8 children bring lunch to school.

4 bring **juice**.
1 brings **milk**.
3 bring **water**.

Help **label** the graph. Use a **J** for juice, **M** for milk, and **W** for water.

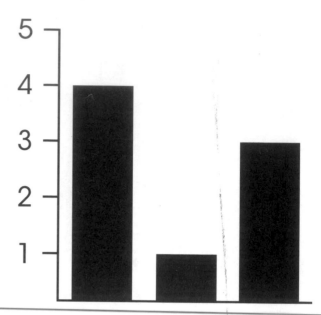

_J_ _M_ _W_

Hint #1:

Look at this graph. Does this help?

Hint #2:

Use the right letter!

Answer:

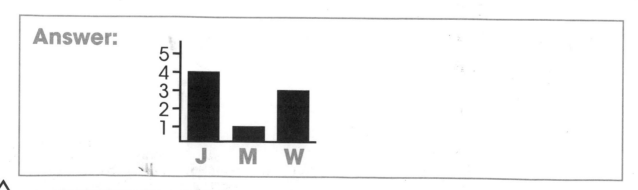

10.

Favorite Fruit

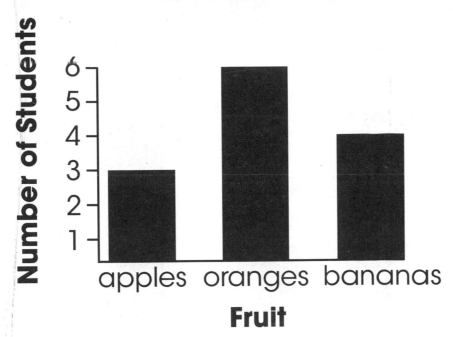

How many kids

_____

liked **bananas**? _____

How many kids

_____

liked **apples**? _____

How many kids

_____

liked **oranges**? _____

See hint and answers on the fo. wing page.

© Kaplan Publishing, Inc.

Hint: Does this graph help?

Favorite Fruit

apples   oranges   bananas

Answer:

4 kids liked **bananas** best.

3 kids liked **apples** best.

6 kids liked **oranges** best.

11. # Fun things I do on the weekends

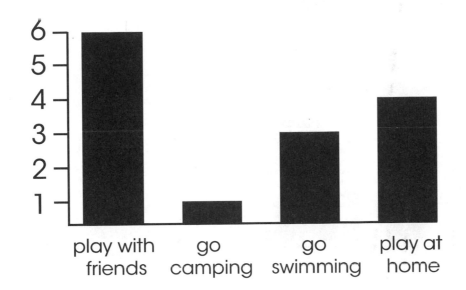

| | play with friends | go camping | go swimming | play at home |

How many children went **swimming**?

_____

- - - -
_____ children went swimming.

How many children **played with their friends**?

_____

- - - -
_____ children played with their friends.

See hint and answers on the following page.

Fun things I do on the weekends

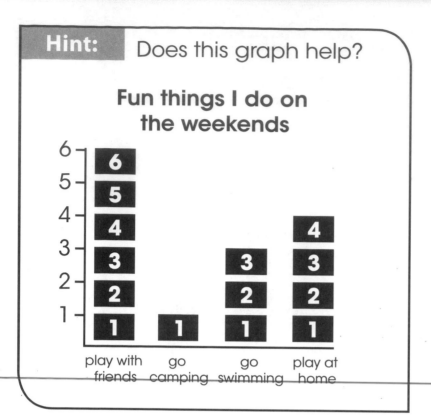

6
5
4
3
2
1

| play with friends | go camping | go swimming | play at home |

Answer: 3 children went swimming.

6 children played with their friends.

© Kaplan Publishing, Inc.

12.

Is the cat **above** or **below** the table?
Circle your answer.

Above

Below

Hint #1:

The girl is
above
the chair.

Hint #2:

The girl is
below
the chair.

Answer: The cat is (**above**) the table.

13.

Who is **below** the bridge?
Circle the answer.

Hint:

She is **below** the bird.

Answer:

14. Circle the fish on the **left**. **Put** an **X** through the fish on the **right**.

Hint:

The **book** is on the **left**.
The **turtle** is on the **right**.

Answer:

15. Ms. Lake wants to open the window on the **right**.

Help her find the **right window**! **Circle** the window on the right.

Hint:

The **hat** is on the **left**.
The **brush** is on the **right**.

Answer:

Challenge Activity

You're doing a great job so far!
Are you ready for a Challenge Activity?
Good luck!

10 children were asked to choose their favorite color.

2 chose **red**.
5 chose **blue**.
3 chose **pink**.

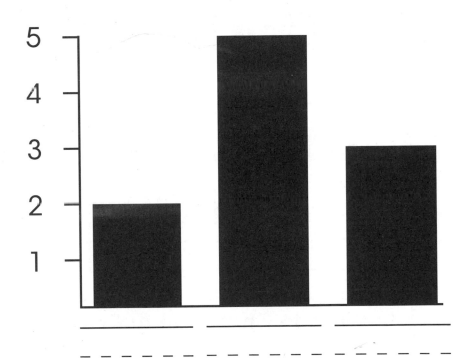

a) Add the words **red**, **blue**, and **pink** to the graph.

b) What was the color that **most** children liked?

_____

- - - - - - - - - - - - - - - - - - - -

_____

c) What was the color that children liked **least**?

_____

- - - - - - - - - - - - - - - - - - - -

_____

Hint #1:

Match the **color** with the **bar**!

3
2
1

color

Hint #2:

Which number is **biggest**: **5**, **3**, or **2**?

Answers to Challenge Activity:

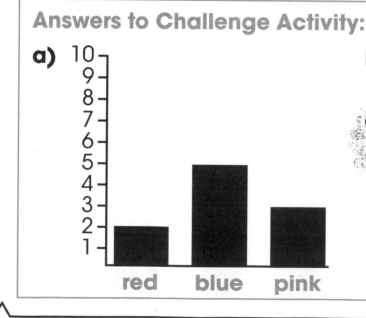

a)

10
9
8
7
6
5
4
3
2
1

red   blue   pink

b) Most children liked the color **blue**.

c) The children picked **red least**.

Let's take a quick test and see how much you've learned during this climb up **SCORE! Mountain. Good luck!**

1. **Color** the buttons with **2** holes **green**.
Color the buttons with **1** hole **yellow**.
Color the buttons with **0** holes **blue**.

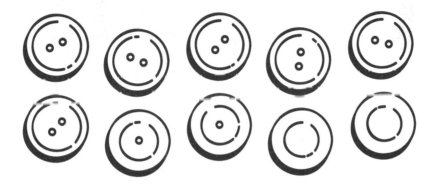

2. You have **3** chocolate bars and **8** lollipops in a bag. Which are you **most likely** to get first?

Circle your answer.

3. Look at the graph.

How many people _____

have **red** shirts? _____

How many people _____

have **blue** shirts? _____

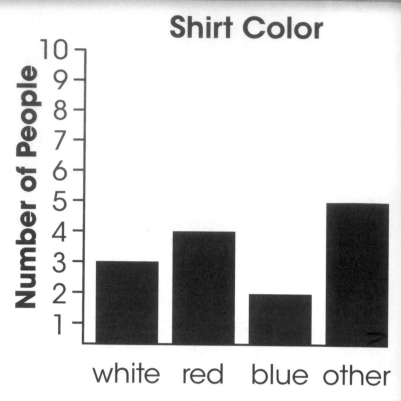

Shirt Color

Number of People

10
9
8
7
6
5
4
3
2
1

white   red   blue   other

4. **Circle** the girl sitting **below** the tree.

5. Here are **3** houses.
Color the one on the **left green**.
Color the one on the **right red**.
Color the one in the **middle yellow**.

Answers to test questions:

1.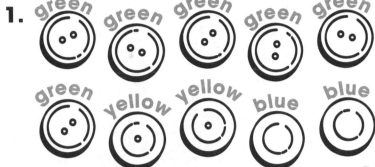

2. You would be most likely to get a **lollipop** first. There are **more** lollipops than chocolate bars.

3. 4 people have **red** shirts.
2 people have **blue** shirts.

4.

5.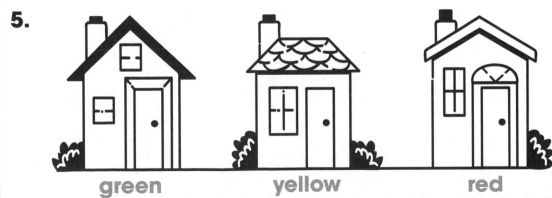

green   yellow   red

Celebrate!

Let's take a fun break before we go to the next base camp. You've earned it!

Let's draw a **fun picture**!

You will need:

- Paper
- Crayons
- Decorations for drawing, like glitter, glue, or stickers

Congratulations! You're halfway to the top of *SCORE!* Mountain.

BASE CAMP 1

BASE CAMP 2

BASE CAMP 3

Directions:

- Get out a piece of drawing paper.

- **Draw** a line down the middle of it, splitting the paper in **half**.

- On one side, **draw** something you see out of your window.

  - This might be a **car**, a **cat**, or a **tree**.

- On the other side, **draw** something that you are **not** likely to see out your window. This can be something goofy!

  - Maybe it could be a **dinosaur** or a **unicorn**.

- **Decorate** this picture any way you'd like!

Good luck and have fun! You deserve it for working so hard!

Share it with friends and family when you are done!

© Kaplan Publishing, Inc.

Base Camp

4

Fractions

Wow! You're getting close to the top of *SCORE!* Mountain. Are you ready for another fun climb? Let's get started! Good luck!

SCORE! MOUNTAIN TOP

BASE CAMP 5

BASE CAMP 4

BASE CAMP 3

BASE CAMP 2

BASE CAMP 1

1. Dante and Sandy want to share a sandwich.

Which one is **fair**?
Circle your answer.

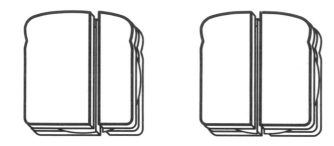 

Hint #1: **Equal** share:	Hint #2: **Unequal** share:
That's **fair**! 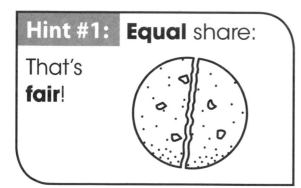	That's **not fair**! 

Answer:

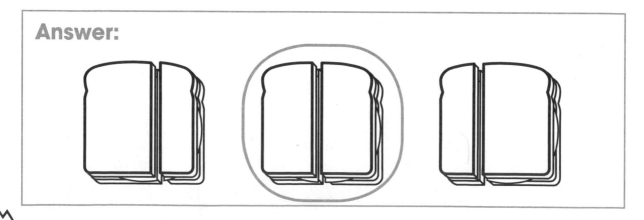

2. Snack time!

Megan has **4** crackers.

Tom has **8** crackers.

Megan has **fewer** crackers than Tom. That's not fair!

Let's give them the same number of crackers.

How many **more** crackers does

_____

Megan need? _____

Hint:

8 – 4 = ?

Answer:

Megan needs **4** more crackers to have the same as Tom.

4 crackers + **4** crackers = **8** crackers

3. Color **half** of this square.

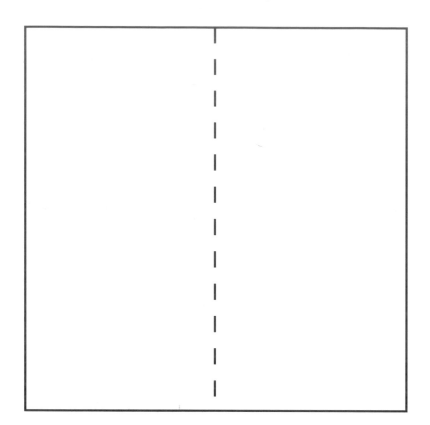

Hint:

Half a circle: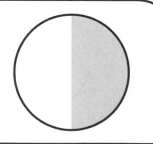

Answer: All of these answers are right!

4. Tanya and Mike's mom baked
6 cookies.

Give them each the **same number**
of cookies.

How many cookies do they each get?
Circle your answer!

6 cookies each   **4** cookies each

3 cookies each   **2** cookies each

Hint #1:

Hint #2:

What number is
half of **6**?

Answer: Tanya and Mike each get **3** cookies.

5. Find the shape that shows
3 equal parts.

Circle your answer.

  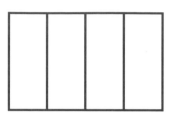

Hint:

3 equal
parts:

Answer:

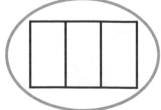 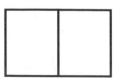 

6. **Color** this flag half **red** and half **green**.

Hint #1:

Half

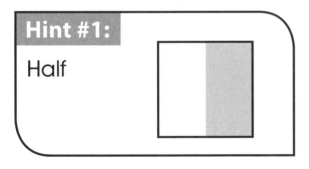

Hint #2:

Half

Answer: Both answers are right!

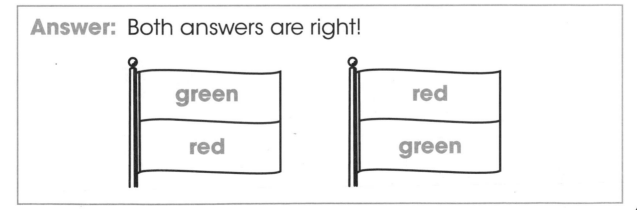

green

red

red

green

7. Color $\frac{1}{3}$ of the sections yellow.

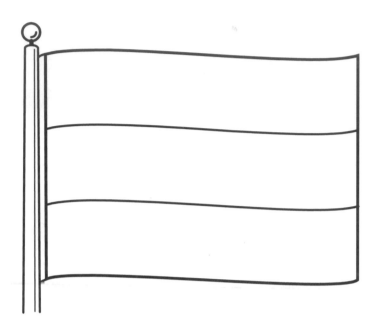

Hint:

$\frac{1}{3}$:

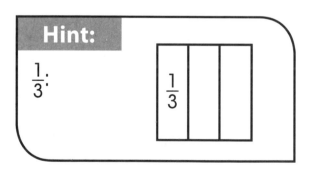

Answer: All of these are right!

8. Look at the shape.
How much of the circle is **shaded**?

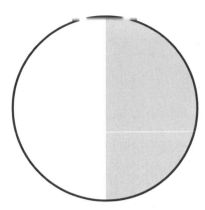

Circle your answer.

$\frac{1}{2}$

$\frac{1}{3}$

$\frac{1}{4}$

Hint:

$\frac{1}{2}$:  $\frac{1}{3}$:  $\frac{1}{4}$:

Answer: $\boxed{\frac{1}{2}}$ The circle is $\frac{1}{2}$ **shaded**.

1 of the **2** sections is shaded.

$\frac{1}{3}$

$\frac{1}{4}$

9. Look at the shape.
How much of the triangle is **shaded**?

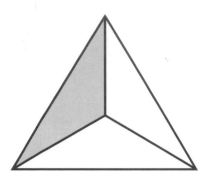

Circle your answer.

$\frac{1}{2}$

$\frac{1}{3}$

$\frac{1}{4}$

Hint:

$\frac{1}{2}$: 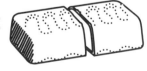 $\frac{1}{3}$: 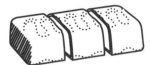 $\frac{1}{4}$:

Answer: $\frac{1}{2}$ The triangle is $\frac{1}{3}$ **shaded**.

$\left(\frac{1}{3}\right)$ **1** of the **3** sections is shaded.

$\frac{1}{4}$

10. Color $\frac{1}{3}$ of the square.

Hint:

$\frac{1}{3}$ means **1** of **3 parts**.

Answer:

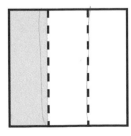 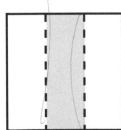 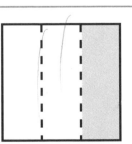

11. Here are **10** bikes. **Circle** $\frac{1}{2}$ of them.

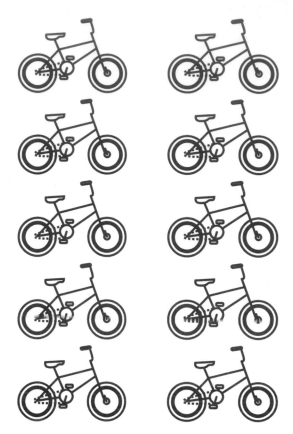

Hint #1: $\frac{1}{2}$ of the coins:

Hint #2:

What number is **half** of **10**?

Answer:

Here is one possible answer.

12. Grandma has a cookie for you.
You want the biggest piece!

Do you want $\frac{1}{2}$ of the cookie or $\frac{1}{3}$ of the cookie?
Circle the **bigger** piece.

$\frac{1}{2}$ of the cookie

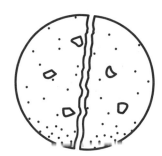

$\frac{1}{3}$ of the cookie

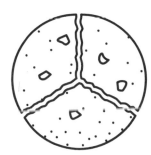

Hint #1:

Which piece looks **bigger**?

Hint #2:

What is bigger?
$\frac{1}{2}$ or $\frac{1}{3}$?

Answer: $\frac{1}{2}$ of the cookie is **bigger** than $\frac{1}{3}$ of the cookie.

13. Circle the pizza that shows **4 equal parts**.

Hint:

4 equal parts:

Answer: Did you find the right pizza?

14. Here are **4** elephants.

Circle $\frac{1}{4}$ of them.

Hint #1:

$\frac{1}{4}$ means **1 out of 4**.

Hint #2: 1 of 4 cakes

Answer:

Here is one possible answer.

$\frac{1}{4}$ of the elephants

15. What **fraction** of the circle is **shaded**?

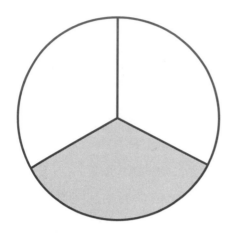

Circle your answer.

$\frac{1}{2}$

$\frac{1}{3}$

$\frac{1}{4}$

Hint #1:
There are **3** parts, and **1** of them is **shaded**.

Hint #2:
Which means **1 out of 3**?

Answer: $\left(\frac{1}{3}\right)$
1 out of **3** sections is **shaded**.

Challenge Activity

**You're doing a great job so far!
Are you ready for a Challenge Activity?
Good luck!**

Will has **12** cupcakes.

a) Which shows how many
cupcakes he has?
Circle your answer.

b) Will gives $\frac{1}{2}$ of the cupcakes to his
friends and keeps the other $\frac{1}{2}$ for himself.

How many does he have left for himself?
Circle your answer.

4   **6**   **8**

c) Now, Will eats $\frac{1}{2}$ of what he had left.

How many did he eat?
Circle your answer.

2   3   4

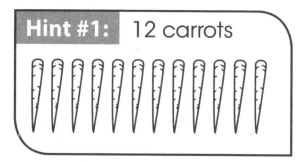

Hint #1: 12 carrots

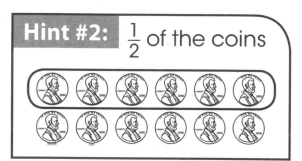

Hint #2: $\frac{1}{2}$ of the coins

Answer: a) Will started out with this many cupcakes:

b) He gave **6** cupcakes away to friends and kept **6** for himself. $\frac{1}{2}$ of **12** is **6**.

4   (6)   8

c) Will ate **3** of his cupcakes. $\frac{1}{2}$ of **6** is **3**.

2   (3)   4

Let's take a quick test and see how much you've learned during this climb up *SCORE!* Mountain. Good luck!

1. Which pie is cut into 2 equal parts? **Circle** your answer.

 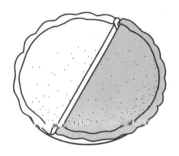 

2. Look at this picture. How much of it is colored? **Circle** your answer.

$\frac{1}{4}$ $\frac{1}{3}$ $\frac{1}{2}$

3. Color $\frac{1}{3}$ of this **circle**.

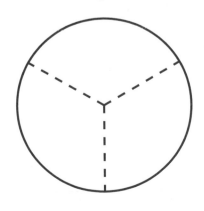

4. Circle the triangle that is divided up into **fourths**.

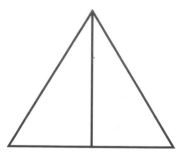 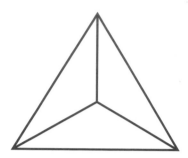 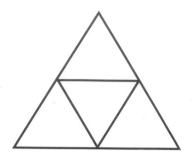

5. Circle $\frac{1}{2}$ of the **8** boats.

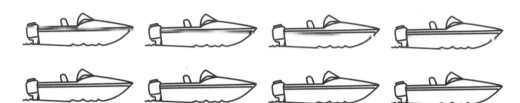

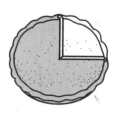  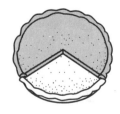

Answers to test questions:

1. This pie is cut into **2** equal parts.

2. $\frac{1}{2}$ of the picture is colored.

$\frac{1}{4}$　　　　$\frac{1}{3}$　　　　$\left(\frac{1}{2}\right)$

Answers to test questions *continued*:

3. $\frac{1}{3}$ of this circle is colored.

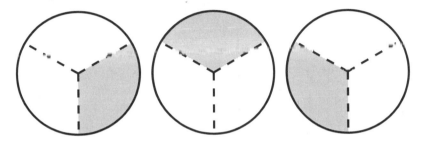

4. This triangle is divided into **fourths**.

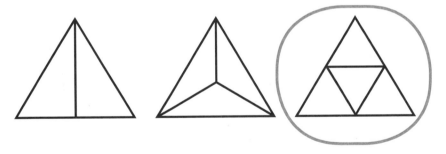

5. Here is one possible answer.

$\frac{1}{2}$ of these **8** boats are circled.

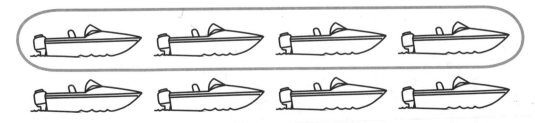

Celebrate!

Let's take a fun break before we go to the next base camp. You've earned it!

Congratulations! You're getting closer to the top of *SCORE!* Mountain.

Let's pretend you are making a magic potion!

You get to choose the ingredients!

Circle what you want to add.

Choose $\frac{1}{2}$ cup, $\frac{1}{3}$ cup, or $\frac{1}{4}$ cup.

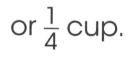

My Potion

 Fly wings: $\frac{1}{2}$ cup $\frac{1}{3}$ cup $\frac{1}{4}$ cup

 Feathers: $\frac{1}{2}$ cup $\frac{1}{3}$ cup $\frac{1}{4}$ cup

 Flower petals: $\frac{1}{2}$ cup $\frac{1}{3}$ cup $\frac{1}{4}$ cup

 Water: $\frac{1}{2}$ cup $\frac{1}{3}$ cup $\frac{1}{4}$ cup

 Vinegar: $\frac{1}{2}$ cup $\frac{1}{3}$ cup $\frac{1}{4}$ cup

 Fish scales: $\frac{1}{2}$ cup $\frac{1}{3}$ cup $\frac{1}{4}$ cup

 Frog legs: $\frac{1}{2}$ cup $\frac{1}{3}$ cup $\frac{1}{4}$ cup

 Slug slime: $\frac{1}{2}$ cup $\frac{1}{3}$ cup $\frac{1}{4}$ cup

Now, give your potion a name! Write it on the line below.

_____

- - - - - - - - - -

_____

Tell a friend or family member what is in your potion. They will probably think it's pretty funny!

Good luck and have fun! You deserve it for working so hard!

Base Camp

5

Algebra and Number Patterns

You are really getting close to the top of *SCORE!* Mountain. Great work! Let's keep going! Good luck!

SCORE! MOUNTAIN TOP

BASE CAMP 5

BASE CAMP 4

BASE CAMP 3

BASE CAMP 2

BASE CAMP 1

1. Is this a **pattern**?

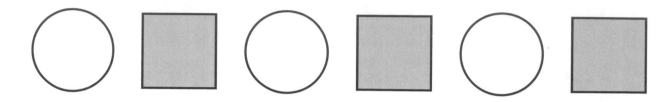

Circle your answer.

Yes

No

Hint #1:

This is a **pattern**.

Hint #2:

This is **not** a pattern.

△ ▭ ▭ △ ▭ △

Answer: Yes, the shapes are in a **pattern**. The circles and squares repeat in the same order.

(Yes)

No

© Kaplan Publishing, Inc.

2.

What comes **next** in the **pattern**?
Circle your answer.

Hint #1:

Look for the pattern!

Hint #2:

What comes after  ?

Answer:

After the tree a **house** comes next in the pattern.

3. Can you finish this row of shapes?
Draw the shapes in the blanks.

Hint #1:

What comes

after ?

Hint #2:

What comes

after ☐ ?

Answer:

☐ ○ ▲ ☐ ○ ▲ ☐ ○ ▲

4. What comes **next** in the pattern?

1...2...3...4...1...2...3...4...1...2... _____ _____

Circle your answer.

A. 1...2

B. 4...1

C. 2...3

D. 3...4

Hint #1:
What comes after **2**?

Hint #2:
What comes after **3**?

Answer: Choice **D** is right!
3...4 come next in the pattern.

5. Is this a pattern?

Circle your answer.

Yes

No

| **Hint:** | Here's a **pattern**: |

□ ○ △ □ □ □ ○ △ □

Answer: Yes, this is a pattern! The animals **repeat** in the **same order**.

Yes

No

© Kaplan Publishing, Inc.

6. How about this one? Is this a **pattern**?

Circle your answer.

Yes

No

Hint #1:
Does it **repeat** itself?

Hint #2:
Are the shapes in the **same order**?

Answer: No, this is not a pattern. They do **not** repeat in the same order.

Yes

(**No**)

7. **Circle** the pattern.

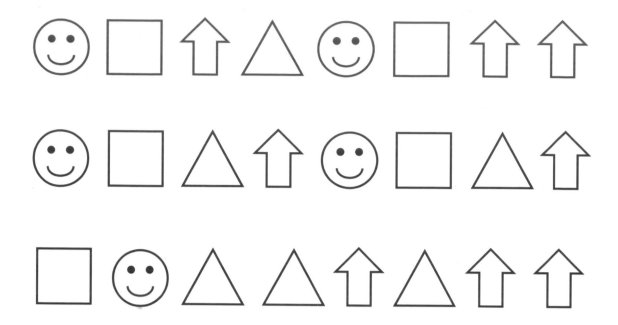

Answer: This is a pattern:

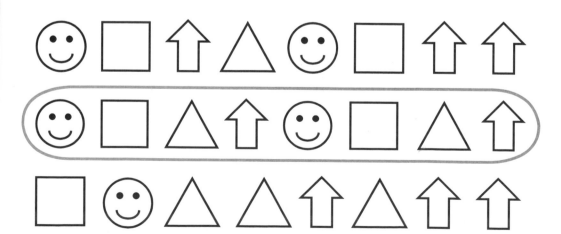

© Kaplan Publishing, Inc.

8.  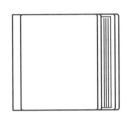   ___

What is missing from the pattern?
Circle your answer.

Hint #1:

What comes **after**

 ?

Hint #2:

What comes **before**

 ?

Answer: The **pencil** belongs in the blank space

to complete the pattern.

9.    _____ _____

What is **missing** from the pattern?
Circle your answer.

A. 😊 ♡

B. ✴ ♡

C. ♡ ✴

D. ✴ 🧊

Hint #1:

What comes **after**

 ?

Hint #2:

What comes **before**

 ?

Answer: Choice **C** is correct.

😊 ♡ ♡ ✴ 🧊 😊 ♡ ♡ ✴ 🧊

10.

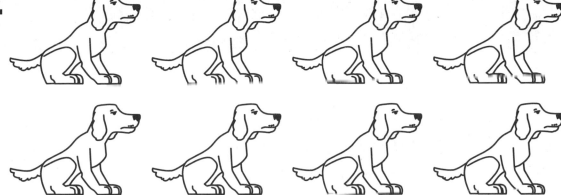

Every dog should have **1** bone.
Circle the right number of bones.

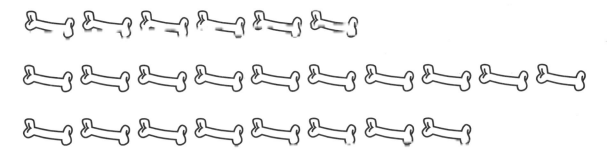

© Kaplan Publishing, Inc.

Hint #1:
How many dogs are there?

Hint #2:
Remember, each dog gets **1** bone!

Answer: 8 dogs need **8** bones.

11.

Every boat should have **1** anchor!
Circle the right number of anchors.

Hint #1:

How many boats are there?

Hint #2:

Remember, each boat gets **1** anchor.

Answer: **6** boats need **6** anchors.

12. Henry has **2** dogs and **3** cats.

Marta has **1** gerbil, **1** lizard, **1** snake, and **2** fish.

Do Marta and Henry have the **same** number of pets?
Circle your answer.

Yes

No

Hint #1:

Henry has **2 + 3** pets.
Marta has **1 + 1 + 1 + 2** pets.

Hint #2:

2 + 3 = ?
1 + 1 + 1 + 2 = ?

Answer: Yes. Henry and Marta both have **5** pets.

(Yes)

No

13. Dana needs to mail these letters.

Every letter should have **1** stamp!
Circle the right number of stamps.

Hint #1:	Hint #2:
How many letters are there?	Remember, each letter gets **1** stamp!

Answer: You need **8** stamps for **8** envelopes.

14. **Count** the balloons.

Do Shana and Joseph have the **same** or **different** number of balloons? **Circle** your answer.

Same   **Different**

Hint #1:

Count **Shana's balloons**. How many does she have?

Hint #2:

Count **Joseph's balloons**. How many does he have?

Answer: Shana and Joseph each have a **different** number of balloons. Shana has **8** balloons and Joseph has **9** balloons.

Same   (Different)

© Kaplan Publishing, Inc.

15.

These children are cold! How many jackets do they need?

Every child should have 1 jacket.
Circle the right number of jackets.

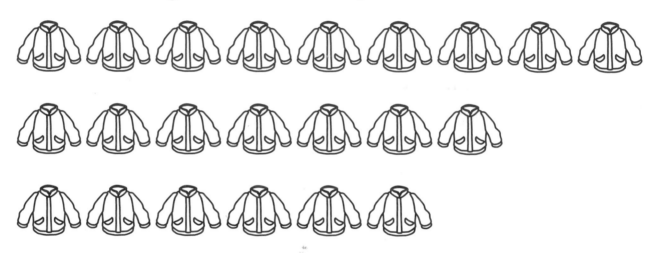

Hint #1:
Count the **children**.

Hint #2:
Which number of **jackets** is the **same** number of **children**?

Answer: **7** children need **7** jackets to stay warm.

You're doing a great job so far!
Are you ready for a Challenge Activity?
Good luck!

Look at the pattern below:

a) What is missing from the pattern?
Circle what is missing.

b) If you changed all  to ⇦

would it still be a pattern?
Circle your answer.

Yes   **No**

c) Is this still a pattern?

Circle your answer.

Yes   **No**

Hint #1:	Hint #2:
What comes **after** ?	Are these the **same** or **different**?  and

Answers to Challenge Activity:

a)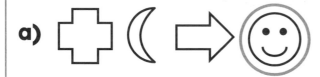

b) **Yes**, if we changed to  it is still a pattern.

   Yes   **No**

c) **No**, this is not a pattern.

   Yes   **No**

Let's take a quick test and see how much you've learned during this climb up *SCORE!* Mountain. Good luck!

1. Can you finish the pattern? **Fill** in the blanks.

2. Is this a pattern?

Circle your answer.

Yes   **No**

3. Circle the shape that does not belong in the pattern.

4.

Each person needs **1** chair!
Circle the right **number** of **chairs**.

5. Melissa has **3** chocolate bars,
5 lollipops, and **1** gumdrop.

Dee has **4** sour candies, and
4 chocolate bars.

Do they have the **same** amount
or **different** amounts of candy?
Circle your answer.

Same   **Different**

Answers to test questions:

1. Did you finish the pattern?

2. **No**, this is not a pattern. Look at the row of shapes again. They do **not** repeat in the same order.

Yes   (**No**)

3. Did you circle the shape? It is **not** part of the pattern.

4. The **6** adults need **6** chairs to sit on. Did you circle the **6** chairs?

5. The girls have **different** amounts of candy. Melissa has **9** candies, and Dee has **8** candies. Melissa has **more** candy than Dee.

Melissa has **9** candies.

Dee has **8** candies.

Same   (**Different**)

Celebrate!

Let's take a fun break before we go to the next base camp. You've earned it!

Let's have some fun! This teddy bear needs your help!

You will need:

- Crayons or magic markers
- Scissors (ask an adult for help with cutting)
- Glue

Congratulations! You're almost to the top of *SCORE!* Mountain.

Pick out **2 eyes**, **1 nose**, **1 mouth**, and **1 bow tie**, and then help put the teddy bear back together.

Color them, cut them out, and glue them on the bear where they belong!

Good luck and have fun! You deserve it for working so hard!

Base Camp

6

Everyday Math

You've made It to the final base camp! Outstanding! Make it through and you'll be at the top of *SCORE!* Mountain. You can do it! Good luck!

SCORE! MOUNTAIN TOP

BASE CAMP 5

BASE CAMP 4

BASE CAMP 3

BASE CAMP 2

BASE CAMP 1

1. Let's tell time!

What **time** is it?

Circle your answer.

8:00

7:00

8:30

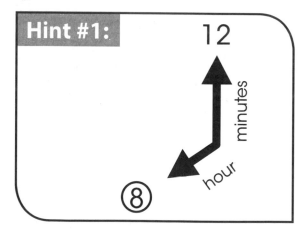

Hint #1:	Hint #2:
12 / minutes / hour / ⑧	→ When the minutes hand is on the **12**, the time ends in **:00**.

Answer: It is **8:00**.

(**8:00**)
7:00
8:30

2. What **time** is it?

Circle your answer.

1:00

3:00

4:30

Hint #1:

12

minutes

hour

③

Hint #2:

➡️

When the minutes hand is on the **12**, the time ends in **:00**.

Answer: It is **3:00**.

1:00

③:00

4:30

3. What **time** is it?

Circle your answer.

9:30

10:30

11:30

Hint #1:

hour

⑨

minutes

⑥

Hint #2:

When the minutes hand is on the **6**, the time ends in **:30**.

Answer: It is **9:30**.

(**9:30**)

10:30

11:30

---

4. Which clock reads **5:00**?

Circle your answer.

Hint #1:

The **short hand** tells the hour.

Hint #2:

The **long hand** tells the minutes.

Answer: It reads **5:00**.

5. Which clock reads **7:00**?

Circle your answer.

Hint #1:

The **short hand** tells the hour.

Hint #2:

The **long hand** tells the minutes.

Answer: It reads **7:00**.

6. Which clock reads **10:30**?

Circle your answer.

Hint #1:

The **short hand** tells the

 hour.

Hint #2:

The **long hand** tells the

 minutes.

Answer: It reads **10:30**.

Let's look at money!

7. How much is each **coin** worth?
Write the number.

 _ _ _ _ _ _ _ _ _ _ _ 　　 _ _ _ _ _ _ _ _ _ _ _ 　　 _ _ _ _ _ _ _ _ _ _ _

Hint #1:

 =

Hint #2:

 =

Answer:

 1¢ 　　 5¢ 　　 10¢

8. Maggie found some coins on the ground. How much are they all worth?

Write your answer on the line below.

_____

Maggie found _____ ¢

Hint #1:

The coins that Maggie found are all **pennies**.

Hint #2:

 = 1¢

Answer: Maggie found **6¢**.

1¢ + 1¢ + 1¢ + 1¢ + 1¢ + 1¢ = 6¢

9. Jack has **10** pennies.

Which is worth the **same** as his pennies? **Circle** your answer.

1 dime

2 dimes

3 dimes

Hint #1:

 = 10¢

Hint #2:

Count the pennies!

Answer: Jack would get **1 dime** for his pennies.

    =

10 pennies   **1 dime**

10. Shannon has

       5 pennies

and    2 nickels.

How much money does she have?
Circle your answer.

12¢   **15¢**   **10¢**

Hint #1: Count the **pennies**!

Hint #2: Count the **nickels**!

Answer: Shannon has ⬭**15¢**.

5 pennies are worth **5¢**

and 2 nickels are worth **10¢**.

Add them up and you get **15¢**.   **10¢ + 5¢ = 15¢**

11. Todd has **2 dimes** and **1 penny**.

Carlos has **3 nickels** and **1 dime**.

Martha has **3 nickels** and **5 pennies**.

Who has exactly **25¢**?
Circle your answer.

Todd   **Carlos**   **Martha**

Hint: Remember what each type of coin is worth!

 = 1¢   = 5¢   = 10¢    = 25¢

Answer: Carlos has exactly **25¢**.

      = 25¢

Todd   (Carlos)   **Martha**

12. Which is the **most** amount of money?

© Kaplan Publishing, Inc.

Hint #1:
Each  is worth **1¢**.

Each (dime) is worth **10¢**.

Each (quarter) is worth **25¢**.

Hint #2:
How many **pennies** are there?
How many **dimes** are there?
How many **quarters** are there?

Answer:
 = **15¢**

= **30¢**   = **25¢**

13. Anna has  and

1 quarter   3 pennies.

How much money does she have?

Circle your answer.

23¢

28¢

30¢

Hint #1:	Hint #2:
 is **25¢**	 is **1¢**
1 quarter	1 penny

Answer: Tanya has **28¢**.   **25¢ + 3¢ = 28¢**

23¢

(28¢)

30¢

© Kaplan Publishing, Inc.

14. Tim had **8** pennies.
He gave **3** pennies to his sister.

How much does he have left?
Circle your answer.

4¢

5¢

6¢

Hint:

8 − 3 = ?

Answer: Tim has **5¢** left.   **8¢ − 3¢ = 5¢**

4¢

(5¢)

6¢

15. Matt had **1** dime.

His friend gave him **2** nickels.

How much does he have now?

Circle your answer.

20¢

15¢

10¢

Hint #1:

 = **10¢**    = **5¢**

Hint #2:

 +  = **?**

Answer: Matt now has **20¢**.

(20¢)
15¢
10¢

 +   = **20¢**

Challenge Activity

You're doing a great job so far!
Are you ready for a Challenge Activity?
Good luck!

Melissa went to the store. When she left her house, her clock said

a) What time was it?

1:30

2:00

2:30

b) Melissa has **2** nickels and **4** dimes. How much money does she have? **Circle** your answer.

35¢

50¢

60¢

c) What can Melissa buy?
Circle your answer.

75¢ 50¢ 80¢

Hint #1:

The **short hand** tells the hour.

The **long hand** tells the  minutes.

Hint #2:

is worth **5¢**

is worth **10¢**

Answers to Challenge Activity:

a)  is **2:30**

1:30

2:00

(2:30)

b) Melissa has **50¢**.

 = **50¢**

35¢

(50¢)

60¢

c) Melissa can buy an apple!

Let's take a quick test and see how much you've learned during this climb up *SCORE!* Mountain. Good luck!

1. Show **5:00** on the clock. **Draw** in the **hour** and **minute hands**.

2. Which clock shows **30** minutes after **3:00**? **Circle** it.

3. **Circle** the coins that equal **9¢**.

4. Pedro has **2** dimes and **2** pennies.

How much money does Pedro have?
Circle your answer.

12¢   **20¢**   **22¢**

5. Which group of coins is worth the **most**?
Circle it.

Answers to test questions:

1. This clock reads **5:00**:

2. 30 minutes after **3:00** is **3:30**.

3. Here is **9¢**.

 **+**  **= 9¢**

4 pennies   **1 nickel**

4. Pedro has **22¢**.

12¢   20¢   22¢

2 dimes   2 pennies   = 22¢

5.

= 12¢

= 15¢

= 20¢

Celebrate!

You did a great job! Let's have some fun and celebrate your success. You've earned it!

Decorate your own clock!

Color the **clock**!
Draw in the **time**!
Decorate it any way you like!

Congratulations! You've made it to the top of *SCORE!* Mountain.

SCORE! MOUNTAIN TOP

BASE CAMP **6**

BASE CAMP **5**

BASE CAMP **4**

BASE CAMP **3**

BASE CAMP **2**

BASE CAMP **1**

My Clock

You should be really **proud!** I knew you could make it to the top!

Here are some helpful tools to guide you through each base camp!

Use these tools whenever you need a helpful hand during your climb up *SCORE!* Mountain.

Shapes

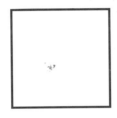 square

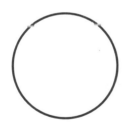 circle

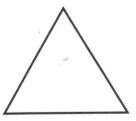 triangle

 rectangle

1   **2**   **3**   **4**   **5**

6   **7**   **8**   **9**   **10**

Fractions

$\frac{1}{2}$ = **1** out of **2** equal parts.

|1|2|

1 2 3

$\frac{1}{3}$ = **1** out of **3** equal parts.

$\frac{1}{4}$ = **1** out of **4** equal parts.

|1|2|
|3|4|

Money

 1 penny = 1¢

 1 dime = 10¢

 1 nickel = 5¢

 **1 quarter = 25¢**

You can do it!

Use these blank pages to work out the questions in your *SCORE! Mountain Challenge Workbook*.

You can do it!

You can do it!

You can do it!

You can do it!

You can do it!

You can do it!

You can do it!

You can do it!

You can do it!

You can do it!

You can do it!

You can do it!

You can do it!

You can do it!

You can do it!
No peeking!

SCORE!

Answer Hider

Tear out your answer hider and use it to cover up the answers on the bottom of every page.

Try to come up with the right answers before looking!

 Ask an adult for help with cutting.